CW00968355

We tend to dread jellyfish, as horrid, squelchy
things that sting you when you go swimming! But
they are interesting animals. They are not fish but
belong to the same family as anemones and coral,
and they dwell in every sea of the world.

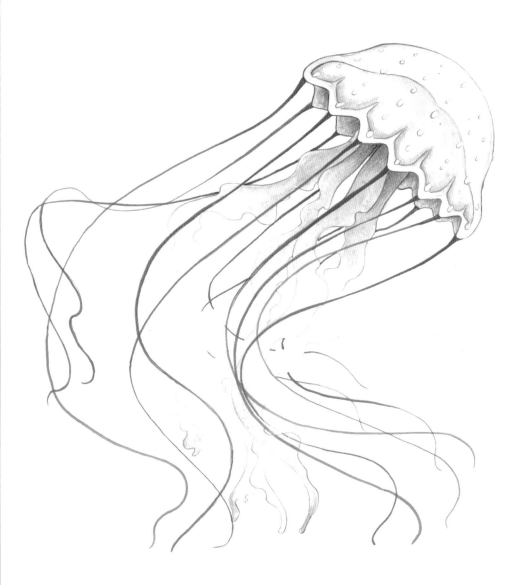

Jellyfish have a soft, boneless body in the shape of a bell or umbrella, with long frilly arms and slender tentacles. They have two skins, with jelly in between. 95 per cent of their body is made of water.

Their tentacles have stinging cells which stun their prey. The sting of some jellyfish, such as the box jellyfish and the Portuguese man o' war, can be deadly to swimmers.

They feed on plankton, small fish,
fish eggs, shrimps, crabs and
other jellyfish. There are some
clever fish that stay in the
middle of the tentacles, as
the stings do not affect
them, and eat the food the
jellyfish catches.

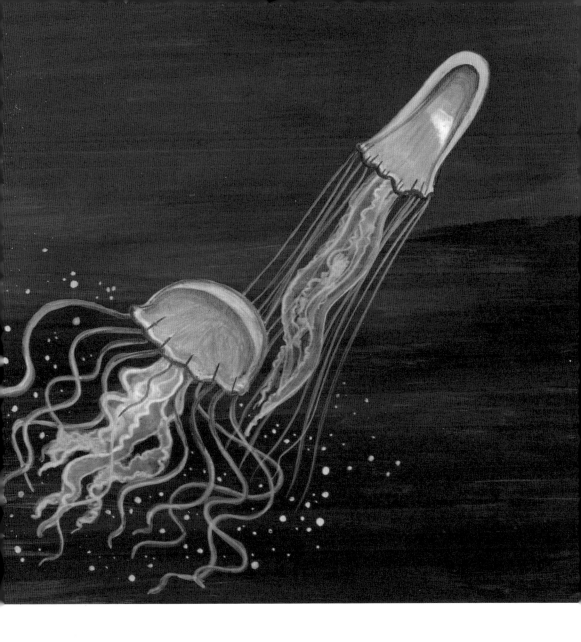

Jellyfish get about using jet propulsion. The bell contracts and forces out water, which pushes the jellyfish ahead.

The 'lion's mane' jellyfish has the biggest span – it spreads up to 2.4 metres across and its tentacles may stretch to 30 metres in length. But you can only see the smallest jellyfish with a hand lens; their span is just a millimetre when they extend their tentacles.

Turtles and penguins eat plenty of jellyfish and people eat them too! In China and Japan, jellyfish are a delicacy, shredded into strips and eaten as a snack or salad.

Fun fact: In 1991, over 2,000 jellyfish were sent up into space on a quest to test how they got on with zero gravity. They came back to earth again healthy but a bit wobbly!